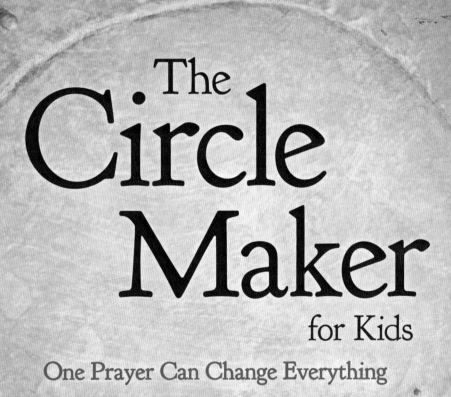

The Circle Maker

for Kids

One Prayer Can Change Everything

WRITTEN BY **Mark Batterson**

ILLUSTRATED BY

Antonio Javier Caparo

ZONDERkidz

ZONDERVAN.com/
AUTHORTRACKER
follow your favorite authors

Dedicated to my children's children.
You were prayed for long before you got here.

–MB

To the memory of Jean "Moebius" Giraud, the path maker.

–AJC

ZONDERKIDZ

The Circle Maker for Kids
Copyright © 2013 by Mark Batterson
Illustrations © 2013 by Antonio Javier Caparo
Published in association with the literary agency of Fedd & Company Inc.,
P.O. Box 341973, Austin, Texas 78734

Requests for information should be addressed to:
Zondervan, 5300 Patterson Ave SE, Grand Rapids, Michigan 49530

Library of Congress Cataloging-in-Publication Data:
Batterson, Mark.
    The circle maker for kids : one prayer can change everything / Mark Batterson
        pages cm
    ISBN ISBN 978-0-310-72492-6 (hardcover) 1. Prayer--Christianity--Juvenile
literature. 2. Honi, ha-Me'aggel, 1st cent. B.C.--Juvenile literature. I. Title.
BV212.B38 2013
248.3'2--dc23   20120401681

Editor: Barbara Herndon
Art direction and design: Kris Nelson

Printed in China

13 14 15 16 17 / LPC / 21 20 19 18 17 16 15 14 13 12 11 10 9 8 7 6 5 4 3 2 1

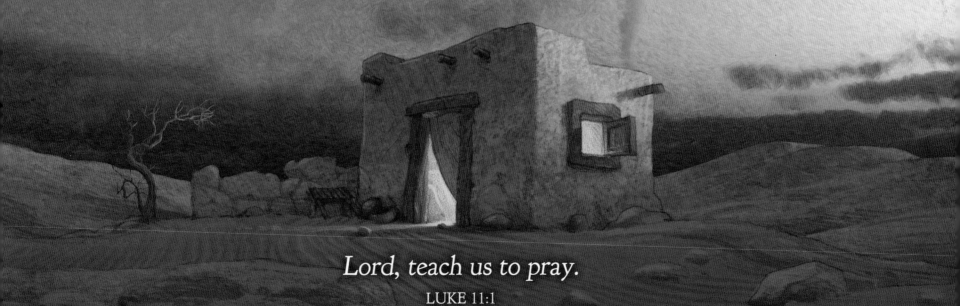

Nothing touches the heart of God more than childlike faith. That's why a child's prayer is so special, so powerful. Children don't know what can't be done. That's why, when I need a miracle, I have my children pray with me. God has answered many of those prayers in miraculous ways!

Prayer is our greatest privilege and our most lasting legacy as parents. You'll never be a perfect parent, but you can be a praying parent. Prayer turns ordinary parents into prophets who shape the destinies of their children, grandchildren, and every generation that follows. But if all you do is pray for your children, you've neglected half of your responsibility. You must also teach your children to pray for themselves. That's what *The Circle Maker for Kids* is all about.

This book will give children an unforgettable picture of the power of prayer. It will lay a foundation of faith that God is able to do more than anything we can ask or imagine. And it will teach a lesson that will never be forgotten: *God honors bold prayers because bold prayers honor God.*

Keep circling,
Mark Batterson

Lord, teach us to pray.
LUKE 11:1

It had
not rained
in Israel for one entire year.

No clouds in the sky.
No water in the well.

Gardens did not grow.
Rivers ran dry.

Dust filled the air.

The people were **thirsty** and scared.
They pleaded with one voice,
"O God, give us rain!"

But when God didn't answer right away,
they lost faith.
"Our prayers are not working!"
the people said. "God has forgotten us!"
Then they remembered something,
remembered someone.

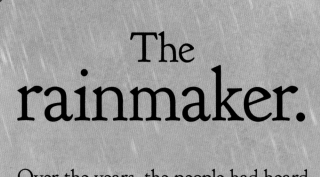

The
rainmaker.

Over the years, the people had heard
stories of a man whose prayers had gone

straight to God's heart,

opening up the heavens with rain.

Honi was now an old man, living on the outskirts of Jerusalem. The people knew that he was their last hope, their only hope. So they knocked on his door, and the rainmaker emerged.

Honi
believed
that even if the people could not hear God,
God could
still hear them.

Then he boldly declared, "The same God who
made the thunder will make it clap.
The same God who made the clouds will
make them **rain.**"

A parade of people led Honi into the city, to the Temple mount. As the crowd grew, children climbed onto the shoulders of their fathers. Others stood on tiptoe to see what Honi would do.

That's when it happened.

Then,
with the
hope
of the entire nation on
his shoulders, Honi dropped
to his knees and prayed.

"Sovereign Lord,
I swear before Your
Great Name that
I will not leave
this circle
until you send rain."

Like water
from a well, the
words flowed
from the depths of his soul.
The people watched
and waited.

Then it happened.
A single raindrop fell from the sky...
then another. The people turned
their heads heavenward.
"That is not enough water!" they grumbled.
"So little rain is of no use to us."
Still kneeling within the circle, Honi continued to

pray to God with a
humble heart.

"Not for such rain have I prayed,
but for rain that will fill
cisterns, pits, and caverns."

Lightning flashed, and there was a loud clap of thunder.

The sprinkle
turned into such a

downpour

that the crowd feared for their lives and
fled to higher ground to escape the flash floods.
But Honi battled the storm on his knees
and continued praying within his circle.
"Not for such rain have I prayed, but
for rain of your favor, blessing,
and graciousness."

Then, like a

cool shower

on a hot summer day,
it began to rain calmly,

peacefully.

The people
gathered together
in celebration.
They had witnessed a

miracle.

Parents opened their
mouths to catch the falling

raindrops.

Children
danced

in the downpour like it was the first
rainfall they had ever seen.
Laughter filled the air.

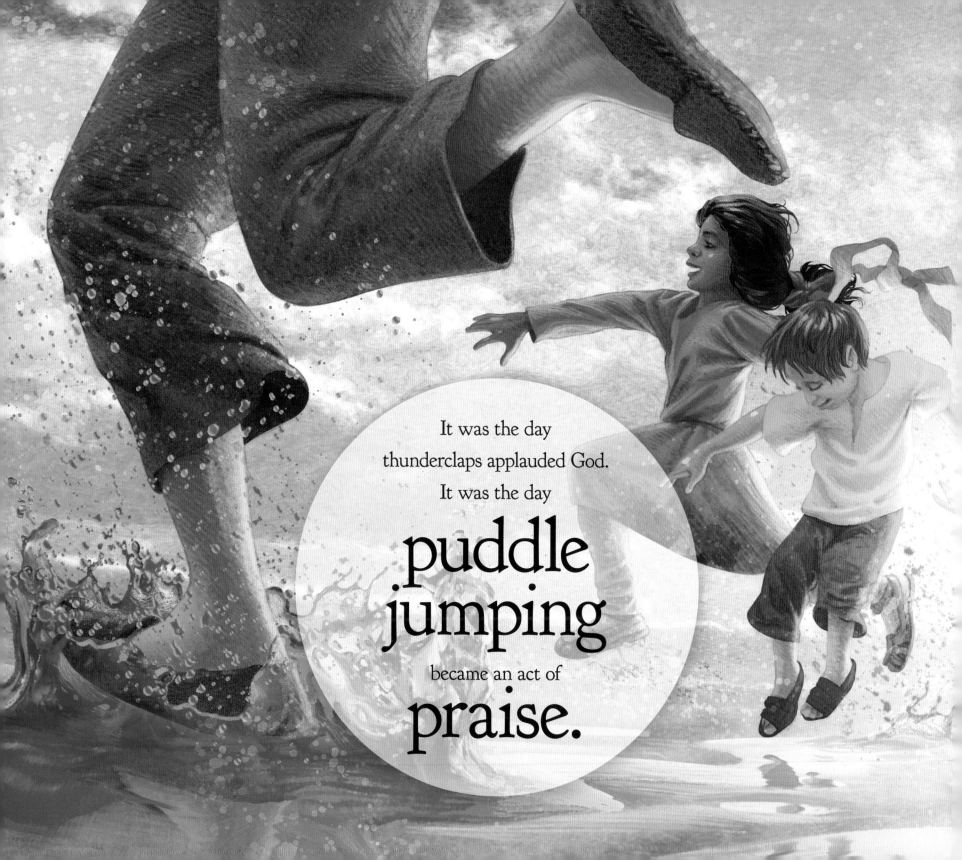

It was the day
thunderclaps applauded God.
It was the day

puddle
jumping

became an act of
praise.

It was
the day the
legend of the
circle maker
was born.

The rainmaker
would forever be known as
Honi the Circle Maker.
The Circle Maker had taught the people

the power
of prayer.

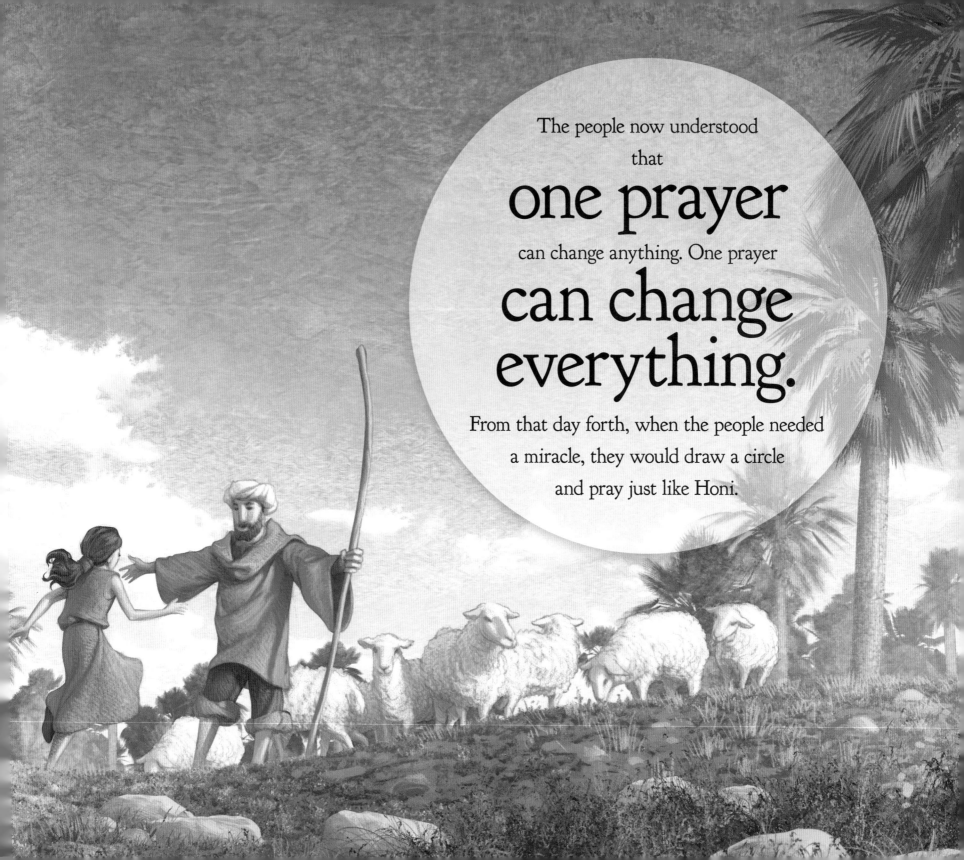

The people now understood
that

one prayer

can change anything. One prayer

can change
everything.

From that day forth, when the people needed
a miracle, they would draw a circle
and pray just like Honi.

They circled the
sad.

They circled the
sick.

They circled the
young.

They circled the
old.

They circled
their biggest
dreams.

They circled
their greatest
fears.

And most importantly . . .
they circled the
promises
of God.

Sometimes they had to pray for a long, long time. But they never again doubted the fact that **God** always hears.

And if our prayers glorify God, **God** always answers.

Everyone who witnessed the **miracle** that day learned a lesson they would **never forget.**

God honors **bold** prayers because bold prayers honor God.